A GUIDE TO THE ANDERTON BOAT LIFT

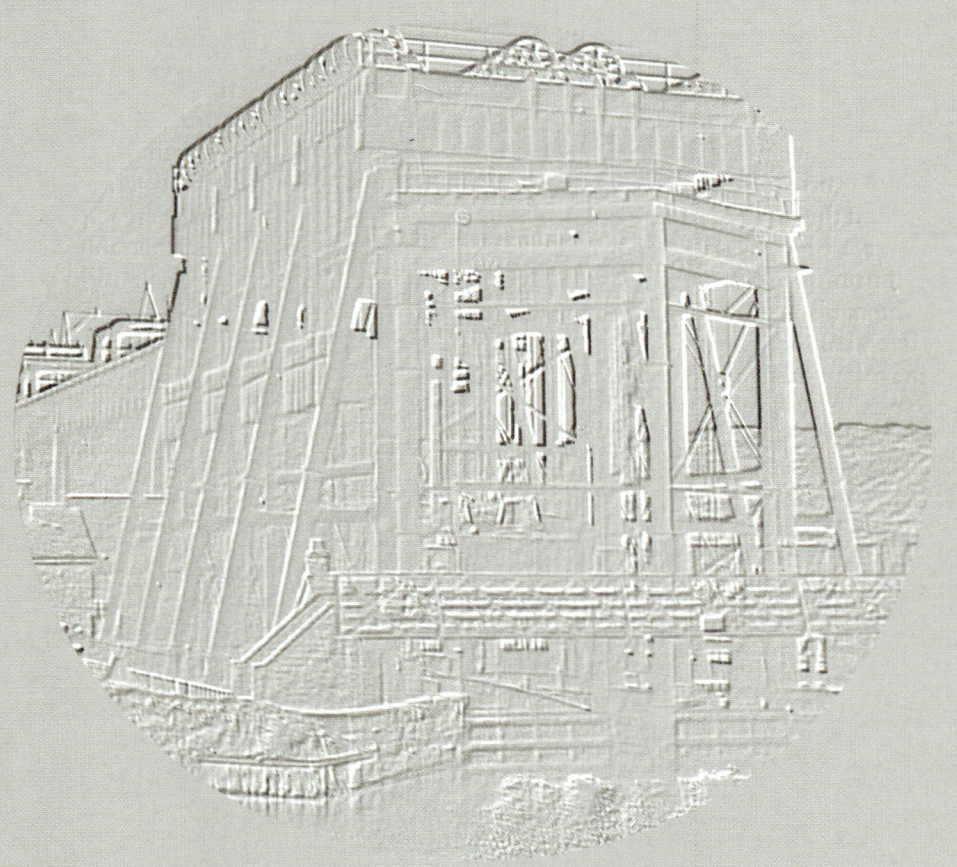

DAVID CARDEN & NEIL PARKHOUSE

The Anderton Boat Lift, circa 1930. From a painting by Eric Bottomley G.R.A.

A GUIDE TO THE ANDERTON BOAT LIFT

DAVID CARDEN & NEIL PARKHOUSE

Black Dwarf Publications

FOREWORD

The Anderton Boat Lift – an enthralling structure – is one of the wonders of our waterways. For those of us lucky enough to have been involved with the restoration of it, the Boat Lift inspires in us an immense pride, especially now seeing it fully restored.

The Lift holds a fascination for those of all ages and many come just to watch in amazement at it work. However, it is not just an historic working structure, for the restored Anderton Boat Lift also has a tourism role to play. The new Operations Centre will allow visitors to get closer to it and to interact with the operators of the Lift.

To fully understand this Grandfather of Boat Lifts, an introduction to its construction and evolution is needed and I am sure this Guide to the Anderton Boat Lift will help you to appreciate its colourful history and to celebrate its new future in the 21st century.

Julie Sharman
Waterways Manager
British Waterways

Copyright: David Carden, Neil Parkhouse and Black Dwarf Publications 2002
Reprinted 2004
New revised edition 2005
Reprinted 2007

British Library Cataloguing-in-Publication Data. A catalogue
record for this book is available from the British Library
ISBN 1 903599 05 9

All rights reserved. No part of this publication may be reproduced, stored in a retrieval system or transmitted in any form or by any means, electronic, mechanical, photocopying, recording or otherwise, without the written permission of the publisher.

Black Dwarf Publications is an imprint of Black Dwarf Lightmoor
Unit 144B, Lydney Industrial Estate, Harbour Road, Lydney, Gloucestershire GL15 4EJ
website: www.lightmoor.co.uk

Printed by Latimer Trend & Company Ltd, Plymouth

HISTORICAL BACKGROUND

Salt mining and pottery making were two industries in the north west of England which had a major impact on the industrialisation of the region. The Anderton Boat Lift was formally opened on 26th July 1875, as a commercial response to the costly problem of transshipping goods between the River Weaver Navigation and the Trent & Mersey Canal. Prior to 1875, the two waterways had been developed primarily to meet the needs of local industry, by providing better transport facilities both within the region and to the outside world; the River Weaver was made navigable principally due to pressure from salt proprietors in Cheshire and salt merchants in Liverpool, whilst the Trent & Mersey Canal was constructed as a response to the demands of the pottery industry in Staffordshire.

Geologists believe that, about 200 million years ago, during the Triassic Period, the part of the Earth's surface which would eventually become north west England contained a large but relatively shallow basin, with a connecting channel to the open sea. This basin periodically filled up with sea water and, due to its latitude at that time (equal to that of the Sahara Desert today), a high rate of evaporation resulted in ever higher concentrations of salt in the diminishing volume of water. When the mixture reached critical density, rapid crystallization took place with the formation of rock salt. Numerous repetitions of this cycle are thought to have created the abundant deposits of rock salt that today underlie the counties of Cheshire and Shropshire. Subsequent climate changes and geological processes resulted in the rock salt deposits being overlain by other strata.

The British Salt Company's works at Anderton, as depicted by the artist J.F. Drinkwater in 1856. The view is looking across the River Weaver and the vessels seen loading salt at the chutes are Weaver flats, shallow draughted craft which could navigate upriver with ease.

A Roman saltworks at Middlewich. This sketched reconstruction is based on excavatory evidence.

Map showing the extent of the waterway network in north west Cheshire at the end of the 19th century.

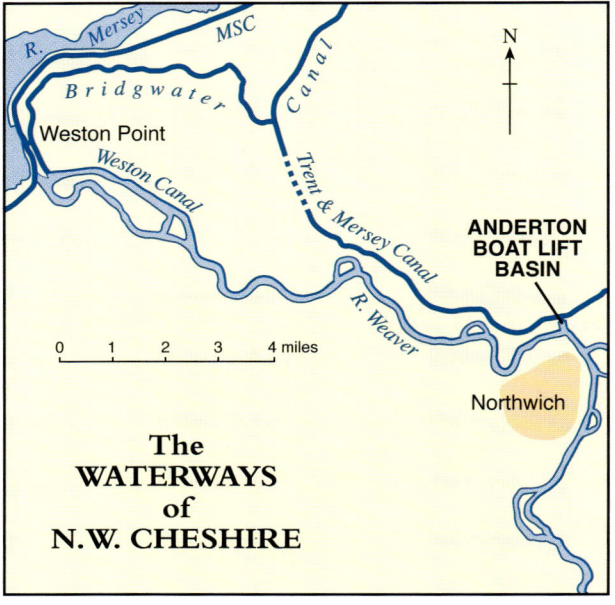

The first exploitation by man of the underground salt deposits was thought to be during the period of Roman occupation, between the 1st and 4th centuries A.D., when water from natural brine springs was used to produce powdered or white salt. The earliest written record of salt extraction in Cheshire is found in the Domesday Book in 1086, by which time it would appear that the salt industry in Middlewich, Nantwich and Northwich was already well established.

Rock salt was first discovered in 1670 at Marbury, a few miles north of Northwich, by John Jackson of Halton, who was, at the time, prospecting for coal. It was not long before rock salt was being mined extensively in the area, both for direct use and to strengthen weak brine in the production of white salt.

Up until the 17th century, salt and other goods were still being transported overland, generally as in Roman times, either by cart or packhorse. The road system at that time was, however, in very poor condition and this prompted influential salt merchants to apply to Parliament for the canalisation of the River Weaver, to provide better transport links. In 1721, an Act was passed and by 1734 the river was navigable over a distance of some 20 miles from Frodsham, near the confluence with the Mersey, through Northwich, to Winsford. Another Act was passed in 1759, which led to the appointment of Trustees to manage the Weaver Navigation and from that time on the waterway, by all accounts, flourished.

Pottery making began in Staffordshire in the 16th century, relying mainly on the underlying beds of Keuper Marl as a ready source of clay. Like the salt deposits in Cheshire, the clay had its origins in the Triassic Period, when large inland freshwater lakes resulted in the deposition of silt. Over time, the silt beds at the bottom of the lakes increased in thickness and thus developed, by the process of consolidation, into stiff clays, referred to today as Keuper Marl.

Initially, pottery making in England was carried out on a local, small-scale basis, in those parts of the country that had sources of suitable clay and adequate fuel for the firing process. As the demand for pottery-ware increased, pottery making became centred on those areas which had particular commercial advantages. The survival of the Staffordshire Potteries was seemingly due to the locally available coal deposits. By 1710, Burslem had become a prominent pottery town, probably the largest in Britain, which, together with the five other nearby towns of Tunstall, Hanley, Stoke, Fenton and Longton were referred to as 'The Potteries'. Today, these towns are known collectively as Stoke-on-Trent.

As local, accessible stocks of clay became depleted and pottery making became more specialised, the potters of Staffordshire began importing raw materials from other parts of the country. By the middle of the 18th century, china clay was being shipped up the west coast from Cornwall, along the River Mersey and the Weaver Navigation, with the final leg of the journey to the Potteries being overland by cart and packhorse. Similarly, flintstones were being shipped up the east coast from Kent, to ports such as Hull or Gainsborough and other towns on the River Trent, with the remainder of the journey again being overland. The finished pottery-ware travelled in the reverse direction to outside markets.

In 1765, Josiah Wedgewood, a leading pottery manufacturer, became involved in a campaign to improve the transport links to the Potteries with the proposal to construct a canal from the River Trent, in the south-east, to the Bridgewater Canal, and hence the River Mersey, in the north-west. The planned route of the Trent & Mersey Canal, as it became known, was from Shardlow, on the River Trent, to Stone, Trentham, Stoke, Middlewich and Northwich, and finally Preston Brook, on the Bridgewater Canal. From there it was a relatively short cruise to the River Mersey at Runcorn.

An Act of Parliament in May 1766 enabled the construction of the canal and by May 1777 it was completed along its full length of 93 miles. Perhaps not surprisingly, the completed waterway was at the time considered as the greatest civil engineering work so far built in England.

Prior to the construction of the Trent & Mersey Canal, the Weaver Navigation profited significantly from the trade generated by both the Cheshire salt fields and the Staffordshire Potteries. Not surprisingly, therefore, the Weaver Trustees vigorously opposed the construction of the proposed canal, as it would separate the Weaver from the Potteries and many of the salt workings to the east and north. By the time the canal was completed, the new objective of the Weaver Trustees was to attract the trade associated with the area of land between the two waterways, to the river. And so, in 1788,

Newbridge Saltworks, Winsford, from an old picture postcard circa 1908. The swing bridge spans the River Weaver at the site of Newbridge Lock, removed circa 1880, and can still be seen today, unlike the saltworks which has disappeared completely.

Salt unloaded by hand into carts from narrowboats on the Trent & Mersey Canal was tipped down wooden chutes into craft waiting in the Anderton Basin below.

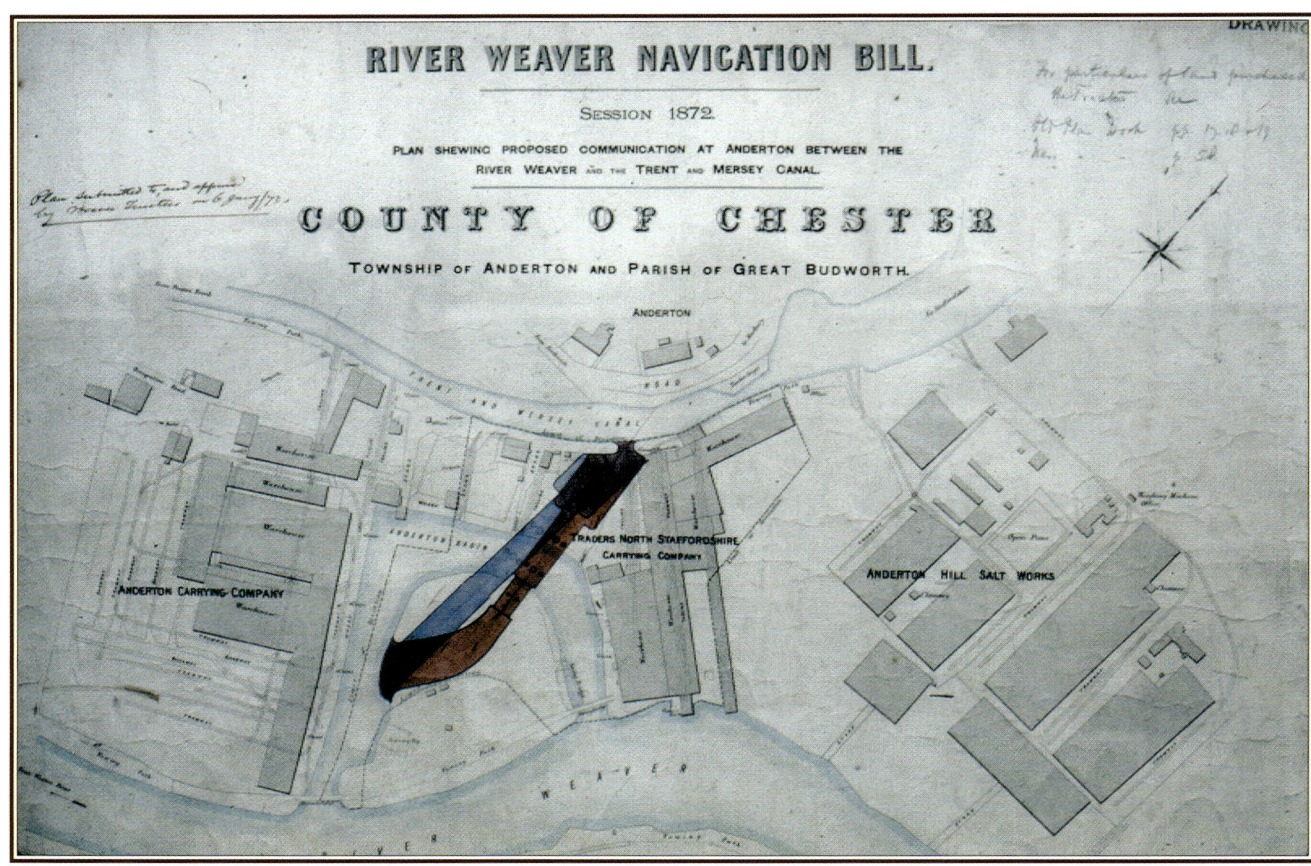

Plan of the Trent & Mersey Canal, River Weaver and the Anderton Basin, showing proposed alignments for the lift, 1872. In the event, it was the blue option which was chosen. Also shown are the various salt chutes and inclines by which means transshipment of salt and other goods was effected at this time, plus the warehouses and works of the various salt and carrying companies based nearby.

largely as a result of pressure from salt proprietors at Middlewich but perhaps also with encouragement from the pottery manufacturers, investigations were begun by the Trustees into the development of a connection between the canal and the river. The location chosen for a link was at Anderton, where the two waterways run roughly in parallel in an east/west direction, separated vertically by a height of nominally 50 feet and horizontally by some 400 feet.

By 1793, the Trustees had purchased suitable land from Sir John Stanley and work had begun on the excavation of a basin on the north bank of the river, at the bottom of the steep valleyside below the canal. Thus began the transshipment of cargoes from canal boat to river boat and vice versa. By the turn of the century, two salt chutes and an incline had been built between the canal and the basin, with white salt being manually offloaded from barges in the canal and barrowed across the towpath and onto wooden platforms, or gantries, projecting out across the river valley; from there the salt was tipped down wooden chutes directly into larger river boats in the basin. Over the ensuing years, further development took place at the basin, which included, amongst other things, the erection of storage buildings and wharves, generally at the lower level.

Initially, most of the transshipment was downwards, from the canal to the river, principally salt but also pottery-ware. However, two cranes were erected in 1796, in an effort to tempt carriers to bring the raw materials destined for the Potteries along the Weaver, before being transferred to the canal for the final leg of the journey.

By minimising the cost of transshipping goods at the Anderton Basin, the Trustees were able to make the route between Anderton and Liverpool more competitive than the alternative, via the Trent & Mersey and Bridgewater Canals. As a result, significant quantities of salt and pottery-ware were attracted off the canal at Anderton and down to the river. This is evident from the records, which indicate that, for the five year period between April 1795 and April 1800, a total of 17,674 tons of white salt from Middlewich was transshipped from canal to river at Anderton.

In 1831, in response to increasing demand, the Trustees authorised the construction of a second entrance to the basin from the river, about 150 yards downstream of the original entrance, with the consequence that a loop with a central island was created. By the middle of the 19th century, the Anderton Basin had become a major focus for canal and river traffic in the north west of England, with an annual tonnage of over 30,000 tons of pottery goods alone being transshipped. Several commercial carriers had established bases at the basin and by 1870 extensive warehousing had been developed around its edges.

The Weaver packet Constance *being loaded with white salt underneath the chutes in the Anderton Basin, circa 1930. Another packet,* Weaver Belle, *and her dumb barge* Gowanburn, *await loading in the background.*

'The Chimney Sweep'. Cleaning duties in progress whilst waiting for a cargo on the Trent & Mersey Canal in the Potteries circa 1920. The distinctive shape of a kiln looms over the waterway.

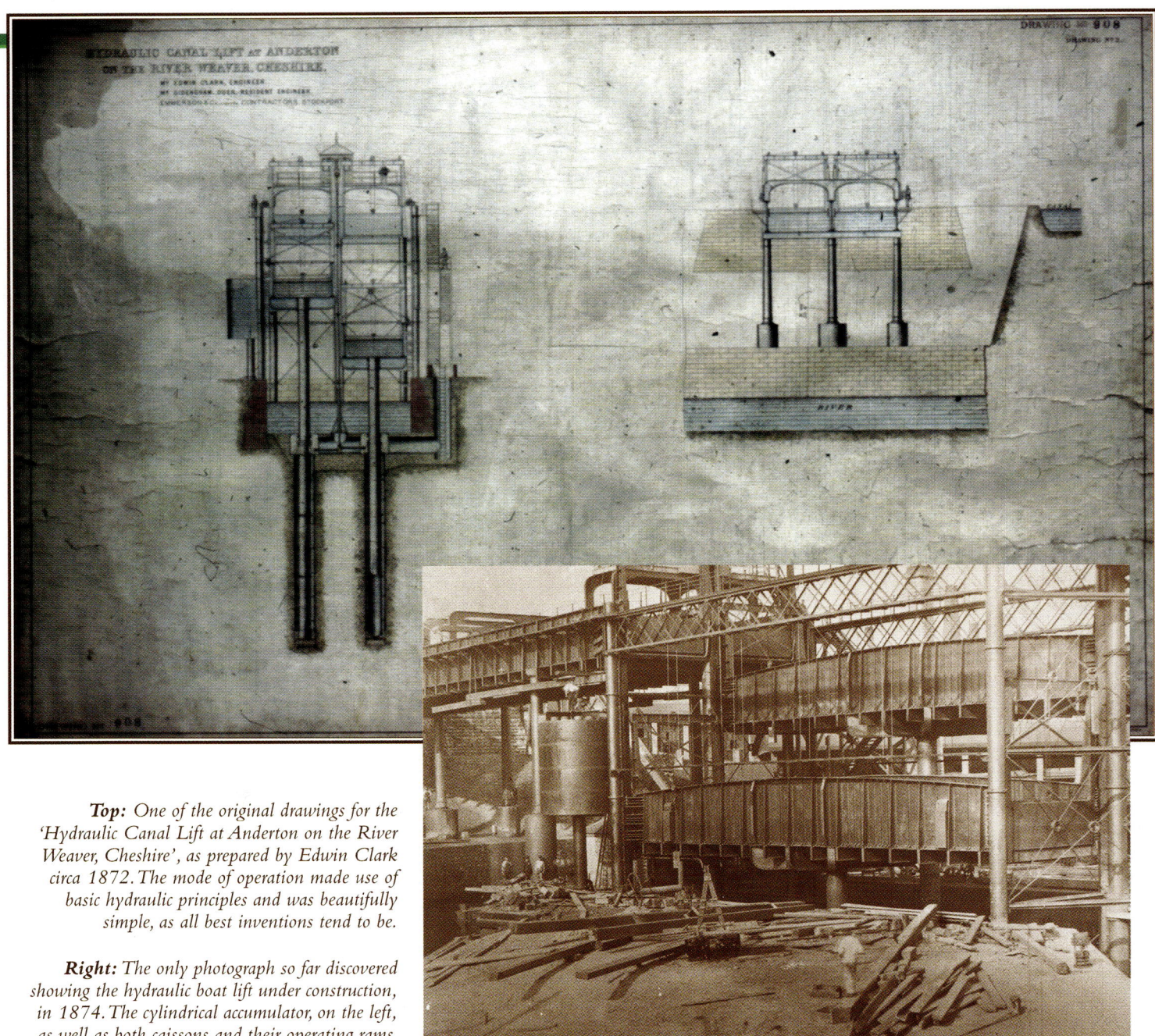

Top: One of the original drawings for the 'Hydraulic Canal Lift at Anderton on the River Weaver, Cheshire', as prepared by Edwin Clark circa 1872. The mode of operation made use of basic hydraulic principles and was beautifully simple, as all best inventions tend to be.

Right: The only photograph so far discovered showing the hydraulic boat lift under construction, in 1874. The cylindrical accumulator, on the left, as well as both caissons and their operating rams, can be clearly seen.

BUILDING THE BOAT LIFT

In November 1871, the Trustees announced their intention to apply to Parliament for a Bill for the construction of a boat lift at Anderton, which, when built, would enable laden boats to pass between the River Weaver and the Trent & Mersey Canal without the need for the costly and time-consuming transshipment of their cargoes. With the large volume of river and canal traffic then in existence, the amount of time and energy associated with transshipment between narrowboats in the canal and river boats in the basin would have been enormous.

Because of the historical importance given today to the Anderton Boat Lift, it is easy to conclude that the lift was of novel design and unprecedented in engineering terms. This, however, would be a misunderstanding. The foresighted Trustees had instructed their Engineer to investigate means of conveying boats between two waterways, including boat lifts and inclines that had been built in Britain prior to 1870. The idea of a vertical lift at Anderton, therefore, was selected only after due consideration of various alternatives, whilst the lift that was eventually built had many similarities with earlier boat lifts.

The first method that was considered for linking the two waterways at Anderton was a flight of locks but this was discounted due to the amount of space required, the time involved for boats to negotiate the flight and the large amount of water that would be lost from the canal to the river.

Edward Leader Williams, Engineer to the Trust between 1856 and 1872, conceived the idea of a lift operated by hydraulic rams and, after consultation with Edwin Clark, an eminent civil engineer and a senior partner of a consultancy practice in London, the decision was taken that the vessels should be lifted while floating in a tank of water. This, however, necessitated lifting the weight of the water in the tank as well as the vessels and so, in order to minimise the power required, it was decided to include two, equal-sized tanks in counter-balance with each other. (It should be noted that Leader Williams is often wrongly credited as having been the designer of the hydraulic boat lift at Anderton. The records indicate, however, that whilst Leader Williams first conceived of the idea and carried out much of the preparatory work for the lift, it was in fact Clark and his colleagues in Westminster who carried out the detailed design.)

On 18th July 1872, Royal Assent was granted for an Act of Parliament thereby providing the legal mechanism for the construction of the lift. By September 1872, a contract for the fabrication and erection of the lift had been awarded to Emmerson Murgatroyd & Co. Ltd of Stockport, at a cost of

Edwin Clark 1814-1894, designer of the Anderton Boat Lift.

Sir Edward Leader Williams, Engineer to the Weaver Navigation Trust, 1856 - 1872.

A Guide to the Anderton Boat Lift

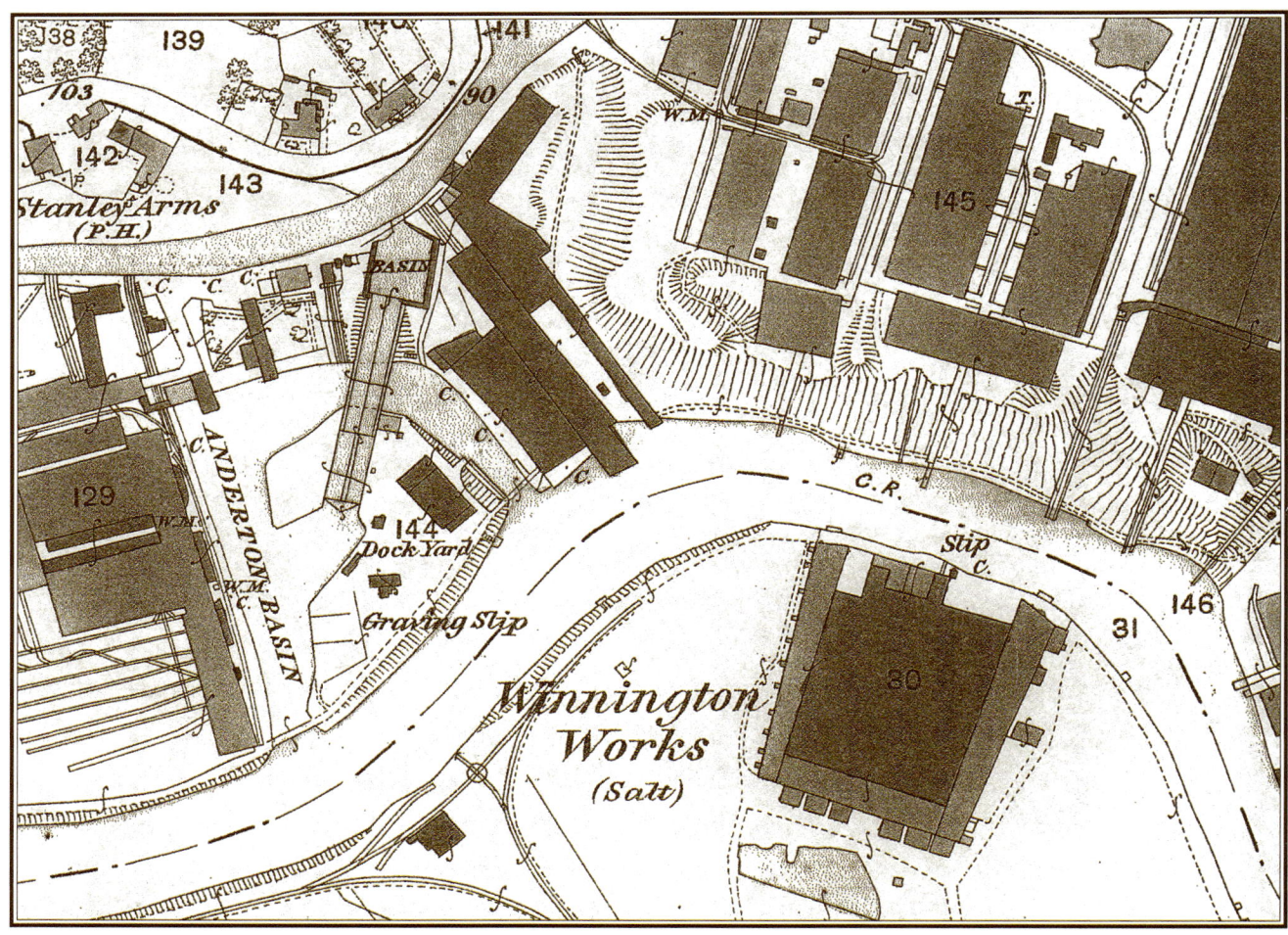

Portion of the 1st edition 25 inch OS map, 1878, for the Anderton and Winnington areas, showing the recently completed boat lift. To its right is the Anderton Hill Saltworks, later the British Salt Company, whilst the Winnington Works opposite, which was eventually to grow to dominate the scene, is still quite small at this date.
Crown copyright reserved

£28,420, a sum significantly higher than an earlier estimate by Leader Williams of £12,000. The main reason for the increased cost appears to have been the higher than expected cost of the ironwork.

Around that time, Leader Williams gained the position of Engineer to the Bridgewater Canal and was replaced as Engineer to the Trust by John Watt Sandeman, the latter soon becoming involved with the design of the lift. One of the most significant changes that he instigated was the strengthening of the foundations of the lift structure, presumably to take account of the high risk of ground subsidence due to years of salt abstraction in the area.

The 1875 hydraulic boat lift circa 1890. This photograph shows a number of narrowboats waiting to go up and salt chute structures on either side of the lift. On the right is the Anderton Hill Saltworks, now the site of the new visitors centre. The chimney, just to the right of the lift, was provided for the steam engine which worked the accumulator.

The construction work was carried out over a period of 30 months or so with the use of extensive timber scaffolding, hoists and cranes (even with the plant and equipment that would be available today, this work would be a major undertaking). One particularly difficult aspect of the construction works was the excavation of the two vertical shafts, nominally 50 feet deep, needed to house the fixed cylinders of the hydraulic rams. This was achieved by sinking 5 feet 6 inch diameter cast-iron cylindrical liners into the ground by hand-excavation, whilst preventing the entry of groundwater into the shafts by the use of compressed air.

The cast and wrought iron elements of the lift superstructure were fabricated by Emmerson Murgatroyd probably at their yard in Stockport, although it is possible that the larger elements may have been fabricated at their Liverpool premises, which would have taken advantage of the better transport route to Anderton via the River Mersey and the Weaver Navigation.

From the records, the works did not run totally smoothly with a number of design changes having to be made. As a consequence, payment to the Contractor was significantly more than expected, to reimburse him for the greater complexity of the foundations and the increased weight of ironwork needed in the superstructure. The final cost of the works was £48,428, an over-run of almost £20,000. Nevertheless, the 1875 hydraulic boat lift was hailed at the time as a great engineering achievement, being much admired for its elegance of looks and simplicity of operation.

The main part of the hydraulic lift was erected on the small island that had been previously formed by the piecemeal development of the Anderton Basin. The island was approximately midway between the Trent & Mersey Canal and the Weaver Navigation, which at Anderton are horizontally around 400 feet apart, with the vertical distance between the two waterways being 50 feet 4 inches. Access for boats to the lift from the Weaver was via the western arm of the Anderton Basin, whilst access between the lift and the canal at the higher level necessitated the construction of an aqueduct over the basin itself. The lift structure on the island consisted of a rectangular, water-filled chamber at river level, formed from sandstone retaining walls on three sides with the fourth, south facing side open to the link with the river. The lift chamber was sufficiently large to accommodate two wrought iron tanks, or caissons, side by side, each 75 feet long by 15 feet 6 inches wide. Each caisson was capable of holding two 72 foot narrowboats, of 6 feet 6 inches in width and a laden depth below water of 4 feet, or a single barge with a width of 13 feet. At the ends of the caissons were manually-operated, vertical-lift gates, which were raised and lowered to allow boats in and out of the caissons. When closed, the gates were effectively watertight so that the caissons and their

Above: The hydraulic boat lift in 1906, just prior to its conversion to electrical operation. By this date it had acquired a larger control cabin.
Below: Side and top elevations of the hydraulic lift, coloured by consulting engineers Lewin, Fryer & Partners to show what remained of the original structure. Blue shading indicated what had gone, yellow meant still present but modified and green showed what was still original.

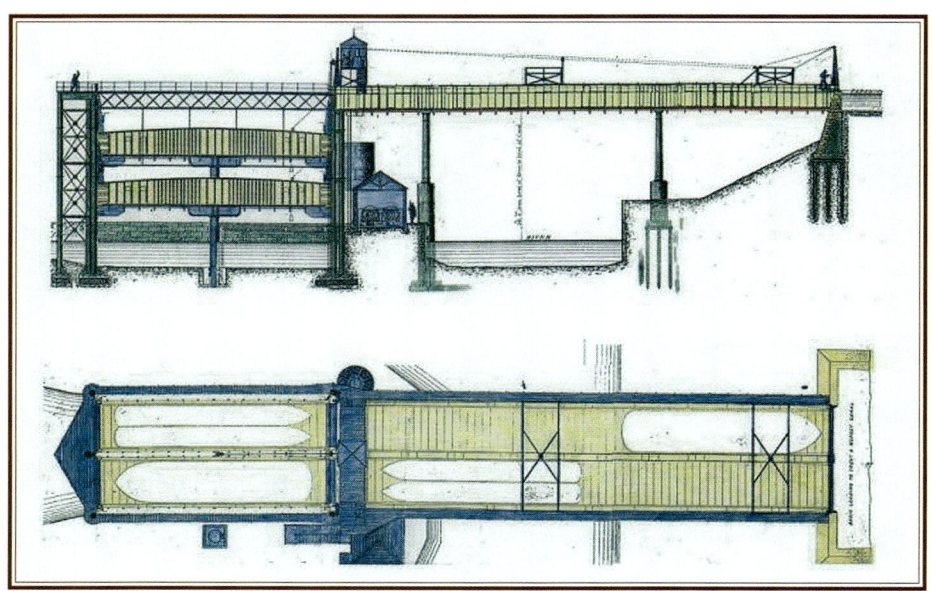

contents could be moved without significant loss of water.

Each caisson with water, with or without boats, weighed around 250 tons and was supported centrally from below by a single massive cast iron hydraulic ram, the cylinder of which was sunk vertically into the ground below bed level. The pistons of the rams beneath the caissons, which were 3 feet in diameter, passed through the floor of the lift chamber and then through a wrought iron access tunnel before entering the ram cylinders. The access tunnel was large enough to allow man-access to the tops of both of the cylinders, the piston seals and the pipework between the two rams. Although being below the water-filled lift chamber, the tunnel was kept dry by means of the seals between the moving pistons and the lift chamber floor.

The pistons and the cylinders of the hydraulic rams were fabricated from cast iron segments with bolted, flanged joints. The cylinders were interconnected hydraulically by means of wrought iron pipework laid within the access tunnel, which incorporated isolating valves and connections to a steam-operated accumulator.

The vertical movement of the caissons was guided at each corner by hollow cast iron columns, three at both ends of the lift basin, with an additional column at the river end to provide lateral stability and to support a working platform above the river entrance to the lift. The corners of the caissons incorporated cast iron guide blocks that coincided with angle guides on the inside faces of the guide columns. The columns were founded below the floor of the lift chamber on concrete and brickwork footings, and were built into the masonry walls of the lift chamber. The triangular, working platform over the river entrance to the lift was linked to the aqueduct by means of wrought iron and timber walkways which ran between the guide columns along the sides of the lift; the platform and walkways being strengthened by wrought iron lattice beams. A stairway at the north east corner of the lift structure provided access between the upper levels of the lift and ground level on the island.

The accumulator, a pressure vessel for storing hydraulic energy, was installed at the north-west corner of the lift structure and was primed by a 10 horse power, coal-fired, steam engine, which was housed in a brick building beneath the aqueduct. A tall, square, brick chimney was built to the east of the aqueduct to disperse the smoke and steam from the engine. Two small brick buildings were built at the river entrance to the lift, one on either bank, for the collection of tolls from boats using it.

The aqueduct, which is still in existence today generally in its original form, consists of a wrought iron water-filled trough with a central dividing wall forming two separate channels, which coincide with the caissons on

An unusual view of the aqueduct from the top of the hydraulic lift circa 1890. The easternly aqueduct channel and the canal basin, beyond, have been drained down, presumably for maintenance purposes. Note also the smaller, original control cabin.

Builders plate photographed in situ on the derelict lift in 1996. It has since been refurbished along with the rest of the structure. Emmerson, Murgatroyd & Co. was the company that fabricated and built the original lift.

the lift structure. The aqueduct is supported in three spans by hollow cast iron columns and it has an overall length between the lift structure and the canal basin of 162 feet 6 inches, a width of 34 feet 6 inches and a depth of 8 feet 6 inches. The normal depth of water in the aqueduct is 5 feet 3 inches. Both ends of the aqueduct could be closed off by means of vertical-lift, wrought iron gates, similar to those on the caissons, which were counterweighted to facilitate manual operation. The aqueduct trough was provided with bracing against the outward pressure of the water by means of external gussets and overhead wrought iron gantries. Watertight joints were achieved between the caissons and the aqueduct ends by means of matching bevelled faces with rubber seals; the latter being compressed as the caissons reached the fully raised position.

A gantry over the aqueduct adjacent to the lift structure once supported a relatively small, timber weather-boarded control building, from which the lift operator opened and closed the valves needed to raise and lower the caissons. From this vantage point the lift operator would have had unobstructed views to the north, overlooking the aqueduct and the basin alongside the canal, and to the south overlooking the lift, the Anderton Basin and the Weaver. As for the lift structure, the aqueduct had wrought iron and timber walkways along both sides to give access between the upper levels of the lift structure, including the control building, and the canal basin.

The final element in the hydraulic boat lift was the rectangular basin, with sandstone walls and puddle clay lining, which connected the aqueduct to the canal. The basin had a narrowed entrance from the canal to facilitate bridging by the towpath and temporary stoplogging to enable the isolation of the boat lift from the canal for maintenance purposes. The canal basin itself, however, was relatively large and enabled several narrowboats to moor within prior to moving onto the aqueduct.

Narrowboats gathered on the Trent & Mersey at Anderton for the Northwich Waterway Festival in 1998 evoke memories of an earlier age when such craft would be sent here to 'wait for orders' – in other words to wait for a cargo. There would usually be something emanating from this busy transshipment basin within a day or so at most.

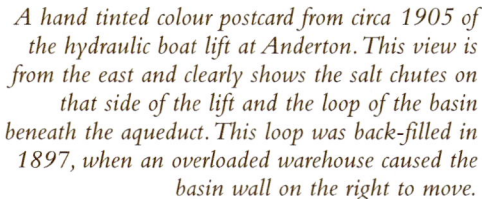

A hand tinted colour postcard from circa 1905 of the hydraulic boat lift at Anderton. This view is from the east and clearly shows the salt chutes on that side of the lift and the loop of the basin beneath the aqueduct. This loop was back-filled in 1897, when an overloaded warehouse caused the basin wall on the right to move.

OPERATION, PROBLEMS AND SOLUTIONS

The main part of the operation of the lift was simplicity itself, making use of the paradox of the 'equilibrium of liquids' as first expounded by Blaise Pascal over a century earlier. Perhaps the best way to understand the lift operation is to compare it to a set of old fashioned kitchen scales with two balanced pans, where each pan represents one of the caissons containing water and boats. Initially, each caisson would contain the same amount of water and, whether carrying boats or not, would be of identical weight due to the boats displacing their own weight of water from the caissons. Under such circumstances, the system would be in equilibrium. If sufficient water was then taken out of one of the caissons to overcome any frictional forces in the system, the heavier caisson would descend with the consequent compression of its ram, whilst the lighter caisson would be forced upwards with its ram being extended. During this procedure, the volume of water in the enclosed system of the hydraulic rams and interconnecting pipework would remain unchanged.

Butty Cuthbert *waiting for the lift.*

A simple and graceful structure. This circa 1880 view of the hydraulic lift from across the River Weaver shows the salt chutes which surrounded it at this time. Note, also, the original stairway between the upper platform and the island.

Barges leaving Hunts Lock, Northwich.

METHODS OF GAINING AND LOSING HEIGHT ON A CANAL 1

*The simplest method of gaining height on a waterway was by means of a lock. The old postcard view, **top**, shows Weaver packets leaving Hunt's Lock on the River Weaver in Northwich around 1908. Larger rises could be dealt with by means of several locks grouped together, referred to as a 'staircase'. The circa 1900 photograph, **bottom**, is of Bingley Five Rise on the Leeds & Liverpool Canal. A true staircase, as here, had no gaps between the locks, such that the upper pair of gates on the first lock were also the lower pair of gates on the second, and so on.*

In practice therefore, consider the situation when one caisson is at the top of its travel at the aqueduct level with 4 feet 6 inches depth of water and the other is at river level with 5 feet of water. The lower caisson would then have 6 inches (15 tons) of water siphoned off automatically so that it contained 4 feet 6 inches depth of water, whilst the upper caisson would be positioned so as to enable an extra 6 inches of water to be drawn from the aqueduct. At this stage, the isolating valve on the pipework between the two rams would be closed thereby preventing any movement of the rams. In this situation the gates at the appropriate end of each caisson and on the aqueduct could be raised, thereby permitting boats to enter or exit the caissons. Once loaded, the gates would be closed and the small chamber between the upper caisson gate and aqueduct gate drained of water. Then, by opening the isolating valve between the rams, the upper, heavier, caisson would descend whilst the lower caisson would rise, the speed of movement being controlled by the rate at which water could flow through the pipework between the rams. The movement of the caissons would continue until such time as the descending caisson came into contact with the water in the lift chamber, at which point the caissons would slow down and eventually come to a stop short of their final levels. The isolating valve would then be closed and sufficient water run off from the appropriate ram, so as to permit the lower caisson to drop under its own weight, until the water level in the caisson was 6 inches higher than that in the river basin. The excess water would then be drained out of the lower caisson to equalise the levels, thus permitting the caisson river-gate to be raised to allow the boats to move out into the river.

The ascending caisson, which had come to a halt marginally below the required position, would then be raised, by connecting its ram to the accumulator, until such time as the caisson floor was 5 feet below the aqueduct water level. The operation of various small penstocks would then permit canal water to fill the gap between the aqueduct and caisson gates and to raise the water level in the caisson to that in the aqueduct. The aqueduct gate and the caisson aqueduct-gate could then be opened to enable boats to move out onto the aqueduct. At this stage, the upper caisson would again contain 5 feet depth of water and the lower caisson just 4 feet 6inches, ready for the operating cycle to be repeated.

The whole operation of moving boats from one waterway to the other could be completed in less than ten minutes, with minimal power usage and very little loss of water from the canal. The actual lifting/lowering of the caissons took just 3 minutes or thereabouts. The time taken compares very favourably with the time of one hour or so that a single boat would have taken to pass through a flight of five locks. Added to this, each boat passing down a flight of locks would have resulted in a lockful of water being lost from the canal to the river.

Under particular circumstances, it would have been necessary to take one of the caissons out of service, say for maintenance or repair. At such times, the remaining caisson could be operated singly by means of the accumulator, albeit with an increased energy input and with a significantly longer operating time.

From its formal opening to traffic in 1875, the hydraulic lift was, in its first few years at least, very successful and was recognised by many as an engineering masterpiece. Although the weight of each caisson when full of water was 252 tons, it was supported from below by a single, relatively slender ram, that had a fully extended length of over 50 feet. The guide columns were Romanesque, whilst the inter-linking iron latticework was attractively lightweight. The mode of operation made use of basic hydraulic principles and was beautifully simple, as all the best inventions tend to be. Only one, relatively obscure, aspect of the design might be said to have impaired the workings of the 1875 lift and that was the adoption of a wet or water-filled lift chamber as opposed to a dry chamber, which resulted in the need for an accumulator to achieve the last foot or two of movement of the rising caisson. (It is of interest to note that subsequent boat lifts in Belgium and France, also designed by Edwin Clark, incorporated dry wells). Despite this relatively minor imperfection, the original hydraulic lift at Anderton can surely be described as a masterpiece of Victorian engineering.

Rather surprisingly, the day-to-day operation of the hydraulic lift was managed on behalf of the Trust by just six men; the Lift Operator, operating the valves to raise and lower the caissons from the control building, a mechanic for the steam engine and other equipment, three assistants for raising and lowering the gates and managing boats into the lift and a clerk to collect the tolls and record the tonnages of goods conveyed. For the first twenty years or so, the hours of working on the lift were from 6 a.m. to 10 p.m. from Monday to Friday, with the men working in shifts. In the early years there was no weekend working.

METHODS OF GAINING AND LOSING HEIGHT ON A CANAL 2

Another way of overcoming rapid changes in ground level on canals was by means of inclined planes. The Trench Incline, **top**, *on the Shrewsbury Canal, was a relatively simple example, built to handle the basic tub boats which were in use on this waterway. Much more sophisticated was the Foxton inclined plane,* **bottom**, *which opened on the Grand Union Canal in Leicestershire in 1900. It saved nearly 70 minutes on the adjacent flight of locks.*

OPERATING SEQUENCE OF THE HYDRAULIC BOAT LIFT OF 1875

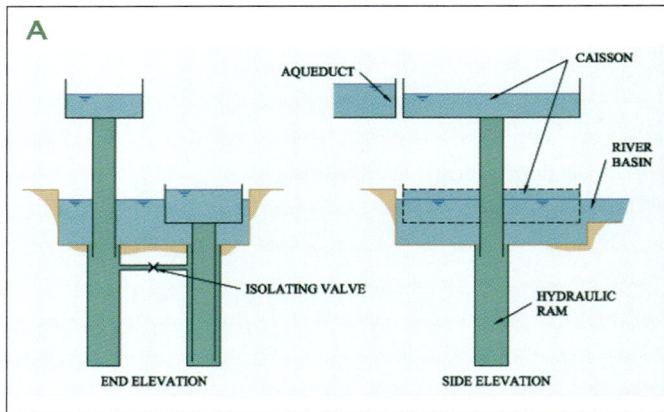

A One caisson is at the top of its travel at aqueduct level with 4 foot 6 inches depth of water, whilst the other caisson is at river level with 5 foot depth of water. The isolating valve is closed.

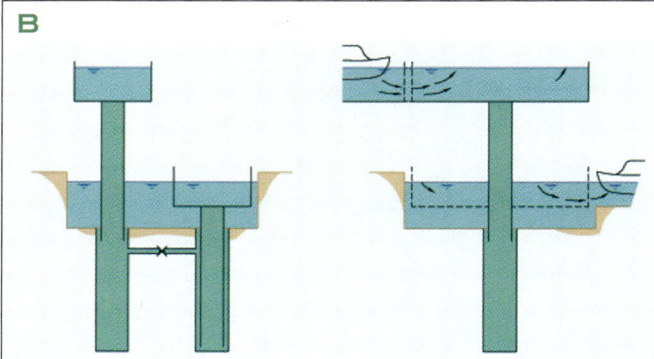

B The lower caisson has 6 inches of water drained off, so that the water level in it is the same as in the river basin. The operation of small penstocks then permits water from the canal to fill the gap between the aqueduct and caisson, and to raise the water level in the upper caisson by 6 inches, so that its level is the same as that in the aqueduct. The isolating valve is kept closed.

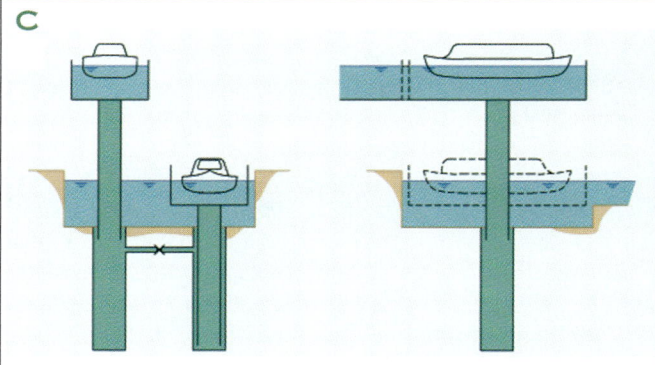

C The gates at both upper and lower levels are raised to allow boats to enter the caissons and then closed behind them. The isolating valve is kept closed.

D

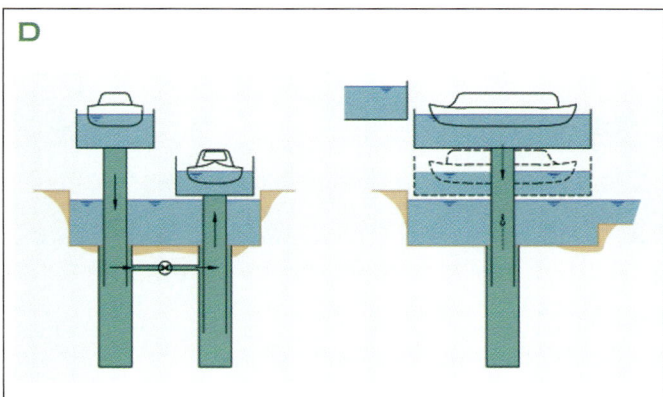

The isolating valve between the hydraulic rams is opened, causing the upper, heavier caisson to descend by means of gravity, whilst simultaneously forcing the lower, lighter caisson to rise.

E

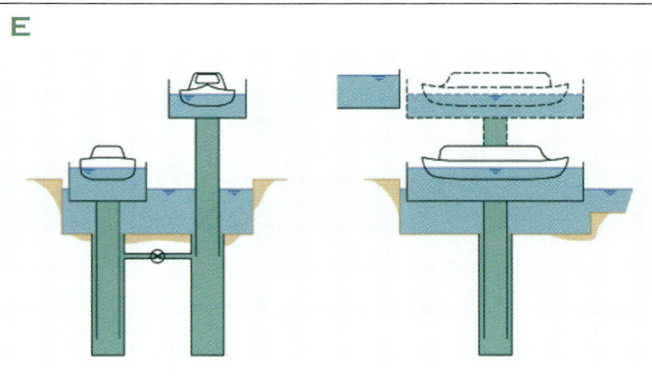

The movement of the caissons continues until the descending one comes into contact with the water at river basin level. At this point, both caissons start to slow down and eventually come to a stop, short of their final levels.

F

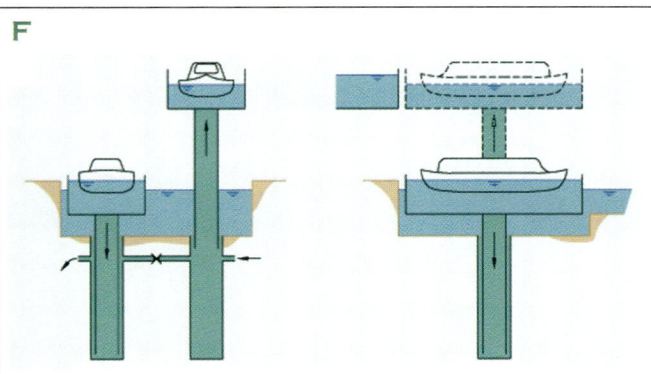

The isolating valve is then closed and sufficient water run off from the appropriate ram so as to permit the lower caisson to drop under its own weight. This continues until the water level in the caisson is 6 inches higher than that in the river basin. The ascending caisson, meanwhile, is raised by connecting its ram to the accumulator, until its floor reaches a point 5 feet below the water level in the aqueduct.

G

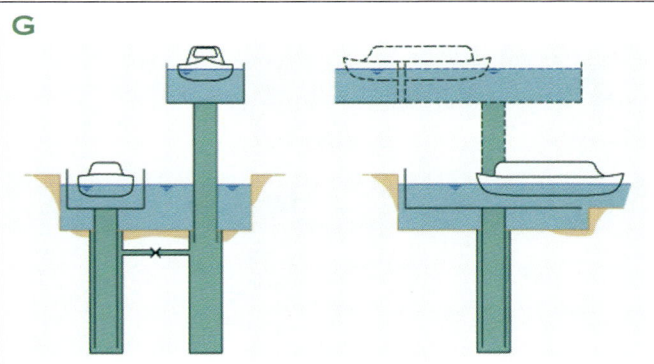

The operation of small penstocks then allows canal water into the gap between the aqueduct and caisson gates, and to raise the water level in the caisson to match that in the aqueduct. The gates are then raised to allow the boat(s) to move out. Similarly, water is drained from the lower caisson until the level therein is the same as the river. The caisson gate is then raised and the boat(s) can move out into the river.

Edwin Clark went on to design a number of boat lifts on the continent. This lift for wide barges was opened on the Neufosse Canal, at La Fontinettes in Northern France in 1888. The old postcard view, **top**, shows it in operation circa 1900. It is today retained as a static monument as seen in the modern view, **bottom**, having been taken out of service in the 1950s.

As might be expected with any new transport link, especially one on which the users were required to pay tolls, use of the lift in the first few years of its life was relatively low, with the greater part of the early cargoes being salt on its way to Liverpool via the Weston Docks at Runcorn. However, as local industry and traders adapted to the improved transport routes opened up by the lift, tonnages increased year on year with only the occasional downturn. Raw materials bound for the Potteries, such as clay, flint and coal, and finished wares from the Potteries gradually grew in importance with respect to the commercial viability of the lift. (Refer to Appendix for a detailed summary of tonnages of goods conveyed through the lift).

The lift apparently worked faultlessly for several years and the first recorded problem was in February 1881, when debris became jammed beneath one of the caissons while it was being lowered, with the result that the cover to the access tunnel was broken. Five months later traffic was interrupted for seven days due to a fracture of the seal between the piston and the fixed cylinder on one of the rams.

The first major accident occurred on the lift on 18th April 1882, when the top section of the cylinder of one of the hydraulic rams ruptured, allowing the caisson to fall in an uncontrolled manner from its fully raised position to the lift basin. Fortunately, the descent was slowed by the restricted leakage of water from the failed cylinder, whilst the water in the lift basin cushioned the impact of the descending caisson, with the result that no significant damage or injury was caused. A workman, however, was lucky to escape with his life when the access tunnel beneath the lift basin was rapidly flooded by water escaping from the cylinder. The lift was out of action for almost six months while investigations, followed by experiments and, eventually, repairs were carried out.

During the six-month closure period, a vertical hoist was constructed and temporary rails were laid up the steep slope between the river and the canal primarily for transferring cargoes between the waterways in the absence of the lift.

Notwithstanding the above incident, the hydraulic boat lift, since its opening in 1875, was a huge commercial success attracting a significant amount of traffic, and hence revenue, onto the Weaver Navigation from the Trent & Mersey Canal. However, whilst the early years of the operational life of the lift had been relatively trouble-free, the ingredients for a more insidious problem were present even at the time of its opening. By 1884, the pistons of the hydraulic rams had become badly corroded due to the heavily polluted canal and river water in the area. It was found that the exposed length of the pistons in the water-filled lift basin had become badly grooved, such that the seals between the pistons and cylinders were being damaged, with excessive amounts of water leaking from the rams.

Repairs were carried out by filling the grooves in the pistons with copper strips. Whilst this brought about a short term cure, a new problem was inadvertently introduced – that of bi-metallic or electrolytic corrosion between the cast iron of the pistons and the copper strips, with the result that the deterioration of the pistons was accelerated. Unfortunately, the Trustees were unaware of the detrimental effects of filling the grooves with copper and this method of repairing the pistons was continued over many years, with the result that the circular process of grooving of the pistons, filling with copper strips, bi-metallic corrosion and yet more grooving, was accelerating year on year.

In 1896, a new problem arose relating to the instability of a wall of the Anderton Basin beneath the aqueduct, which threatened the integrity of the valley side and the canal itself. The cause was identified as overloading of the basin wall by too much material being stored in a private warehouse beneath the aqueduct. To resolve the matter, the warehouse was demolished and the ground stabilised by filling the section of the basin beneath the aqueduct. And so it was, that the looped basin which had been developed some 50 years earlier was reduced to two separate arms, one to the east and the other to the west of the lift.

In 1897, in an effort to deal with the ongoing problem of corrosion of the pistons, the hydraulic system was modified so that the rams operated on distilled water rather than the polluted water from the river and canal. This was achieved by the conversion of the steam engine to compound operation and the addition of a surface condenser. Despite the conversion, corrosion of the rams and pipework continued to be a problem. The poor condition of the hydraulic system, with the need for frequent repairs often with prolonged stoppages to traffic on the lift, was becoming a major concern to the Trustees.

By 1904, the situation had become so bad that Colonel J. A. Saner, then Engineer to the Trust, prepared a comprehensive report to the Trustees recommending radical measures to deal with the bi-metallic corrosion problem once and for all. His proposal was to convert the lift from hydraulic to electrical operation, thereby doing away with the rams altogether. The Trustees faced a real dilemma; how to carry out the conversion or replacement of the lift whilst maintaining the valuable income from the traffic that passed through it. Saner came to their rescue by advising that his proposal to convert the lift to electrical operation could be carried out with just three, relatively short stoppages in traffic.

It was not until early 1906, however, that the Trustees took the inevitable

*Clark was also involved with the design of four lifts on the Canal du Centre at La Louviere in Belgium, opened between 1888 and 1917. These recent views show a boat leaving Lift No. 1, **top**, and the sylvan surroundings of Lift No. 3, **bottom**. The four lifts, which remain in their original working condition, were granted World Heritage status in 1998 but are now bypassed for commercial use by a huge single chamber lift. Although Lift No. 1 was badly damaged in an accident in January 2002, work on repairing it using traditional methods and materials and to be carried out by the Eiffel company, commenced in the summer of 2005, with completion due by the end of 2006.*

Col. J. A. Saner, Engineer to the Weaver Navigation Trust, 1887-1934.

Conversion work approaching completion in 1908. This view shows clearly how the supporting structure for the new headgear was built over the top of the old lift.

decision to proceed with the conversion works. Unlike the original construction works in 1875, the conversion works were carried out principally by the Weaver Navigation's own workforce under the close supervision of Saner. One of the first tasks was the alteration of the lift basin and strengthening of the foundations, which were carried out on a 24-hour basis, with relays of men, during a 19 day stoppage to traffic on the lift in April 1906. A second stoppage, this time of 10 days in August 1906, saw the completion of the preparatory work that was affected by river levels, including the installation of the wrought iron frames for gates at the river entrance to keep water out of the new dry well. There were no further stoppages to traffic between September 1906 and April 1908, during which period the conversion works progressed with the construction below ground of the concrete foundations for new 'A' frame columns along each side of the lift basin. This work could be carried out in a more leisurely fashion, as it did not interfere with the traffic on the lift. Meanwhile at the Weaver Navigation Yard at Northwich, the various steel components for the superstructure were being prepared in readiness for installation. When ready, the new components were transported the short distance to Anderton and, soon after, the five pairs of 'A' frames and the upper machinery deck were erected over the ageing hydraulic lift while it was still in operation. The third and final stoppage was for 20 days in April and May 1908, for the modification of the eastern caisson with the removal of the ram head, and the installation of the wire lifting ropes and cast iron counterweights.

Between May and July 1908, the traffic through the lift was conveyed solely by the eastern, electrically operated caisson, enabling the western caisson to be converted without further stoppages. The fully converted lift was formally opened by the Chairman of the Trust, Sir Joseph Verdin, Bart, at a ceremony on 29th July 1908 in the presence of 40 invited guests. The eventual cost of the conversion works was £25,869.

Saner had achieved what he had set out to do. He had masterminded the conversion of the Anderton Boat Lift from hydraulic to electrical operation over a period of nominally 27 months, and as promised, with just three stoppages to the flow of traffic through the lift. Whilst the converted lift cannot be claimed to be elegant in architectural terms, it certainly stands as testimony to Saner's engineering management skills.

The converted boat lift in 1908, as it can generally be seen today, effectively consists of two structures in one; the 1875 lift, with many of its elements intact, straddled by the heavier 1908 structure. The sole function of the new massive iron and steel structure was to support the heavy cast iron winding gear 60 feet or so above the lift basin, enabling the caissons and counterweights to be suspended below on wire ropes. As was the case for the 1875 lift, each caisson in operational condition weighed nominally 252 tons but in the converted lift each was balanced by 18 cast iron counterweights, weighing nominally 14 tons each, which hung down the outer sides of the lift structure on wire ropes. When a caisson was fully raised the counterweights were at ground level; when the caisson was at its lowest point in the lift basin, the counterweights were close to the underside of the machinery deck. Each counterweight was suspended from at least two wire ropes; one passing over a pulley on the machinery deck at the top of the 1908 structure and then vertically downwards to the outside edge of the caisson; the other passing over two pulleys and then vertically downwards before being connected to the inside edge of the caisson. Every second counterweight had two additional ropes which, instead of being connected to the caisson, were fastened to the pulley immediately overhead. Under normal operational conditions, these ropes were slack with all the weight of the caisson and counterweights being taken by the other ropes. However, in the event of accidental slippage of the working ropes over the pulleys the slack in the spare ropes would be taken up with the result that the weight of the affected counterweights would effectively be taken out of the equation, thereby, hopefully, preventing further slippage.

The movement of each caisson was powered by a 30 horse power electric motor operating through cast iron gears and worm wheels to achieve a relatively slow rotation of the main drive pulleys of 0.5 r.p.m. By this means, the caissons were raised and lowered at a speed of about 9 feet/minute, with the consequence that the journey time for a boat between the river and canal, allowing for opening and closing the various gates and movement of the boat into and out of the caisson, took 10 to 12 minutes. Due to the gross weight of the counterweights being the same as the operational weight of the caisson, the only power required from the electric motors was that needed to overcome the friction of the pulleys on their bearings, the losses within the gearings and other minor losses.

The entire operation of the converted electrical lift and gates could now be carried out in a larger control building above the aqueduct by means of so-called tram controllers. Unlike the balanced arrangement for the 1875 hydraulic lift, the caissons on the converted lift operated independently from

Various stages in the conversion of the boat lift; rebuilding the caisson chambers, **top**, *fitting the headgear,* **middle**, *and one of the outer steel support beams being positioned,* **bottom**.

Conversion works approaching completion in 1908. The new frame and most of the headgear is in place but the original structure can be clearly seen inside it. Clark's 1875 design was dwarfed by the new lift. One of the salt chutes features on the right, partially obscuring the work going on behind.

Side, front and top elevations of the hydraulic lift. The drawing shows the larger control cabin, which dates from around 1902, when the lift gates were converted to electrical operation and other works carried out.

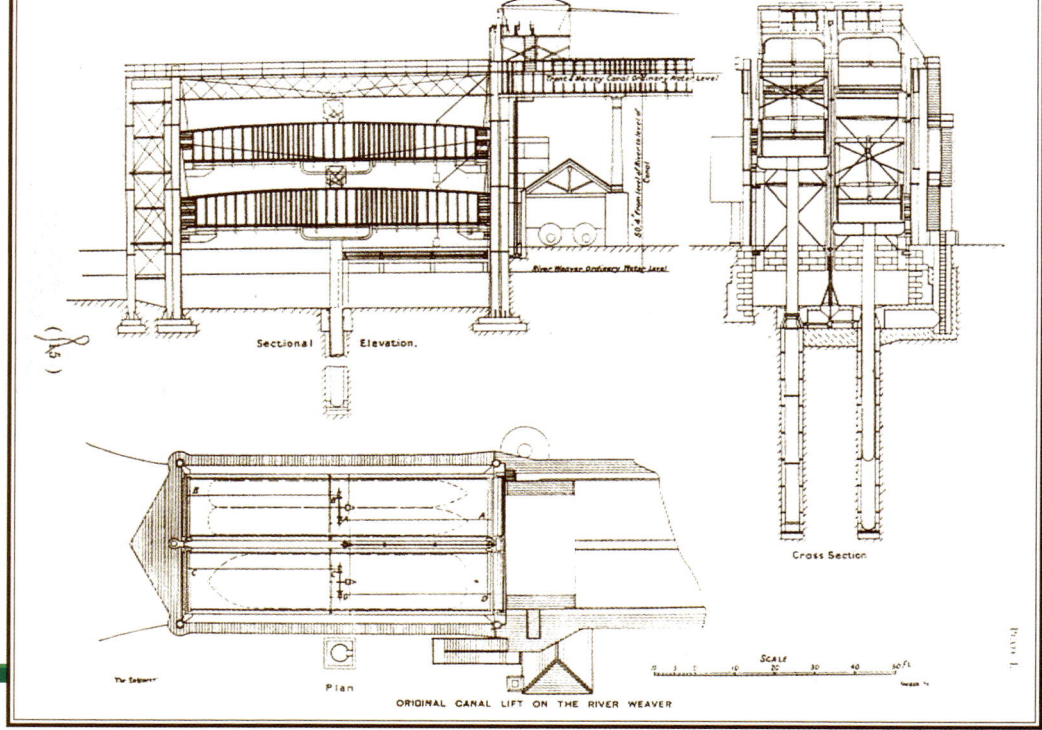

The photographer probably stood on the top of the salt chute seen in the previous picture to take this picture of the conversion works circa 1908. What should be appreciated when looking at the refurbished lift today, is that the massive girders, frames and headgear for the new lift were all lifted into place by means of wooden derricks and steam cranes.

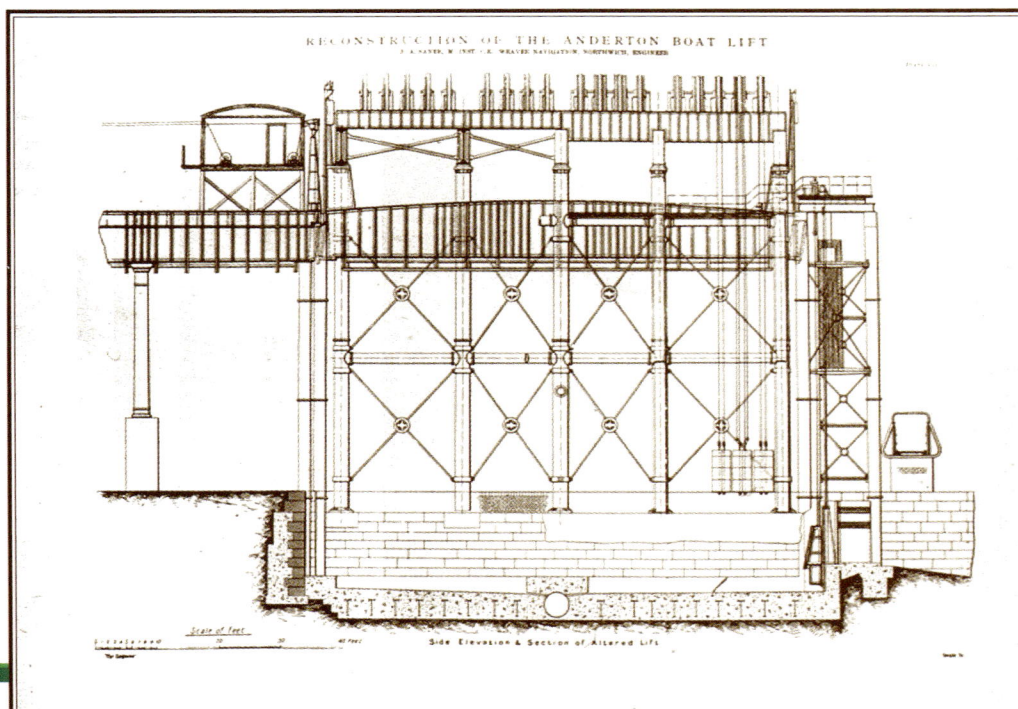

Side elevation of the converted lift of 1908, which also gives an indication of the new dry well the caissons descended into; the hydraulic lift had a wet well, being filled with river water.

This superb view of the converted boat lift was probably taken in late 1908, shortly after completion of the work. The 'A' frames, which supported the massive bulk of the new upper deck, stand out clearly. Electrical operation entailed a whole new system of gearwheels, mounted on the upper deck, working the pulleys and ropes which festoon the sides of the converted lift. The steel footbridge across the entrance gates was also new. Saner's achievement was to build this enormous structure with only minimal disruption to the traffic using the lift.

each other, enabling one of the caissons to be taken out of operation at times of low traffic volumes and for maintenance or repair purposes. Furthermore, the conversion allowed a reduction in the workforce employed on the lift. Since 1896, when electrical power was first introduced to operate the gates, the lift required three men full-time with a fourth man in part-time attendance. With the new set-up, only two men were needed on a full-time basis, one at the upper (control building and machinery deck) level and the other at ground level. A third man was thought necessary, however, to act as cover in the event of illness. He was otherwise employed assisting boats in and out of the caissons and maintaining the machinery.

By all accounts, the conversion of the Anderton Boat Lift from hydraulic to electrical operation was a resounding success. Within just one year of its opening, the total tonnage transported by the electrical lift had exceeded the pre-conversion peak of 192,181 tons in 1906 and within just five years the annual tonnage had risen to 225,000 tons. However, the growth was only relatively short-lived and traffic volumes began to decline at the onset of the First World War and, apart from a relatively brief resurgence during the 1920s, the downward trend continued up to the start of the Second World War and beyond.

Not long after the opening of the converted lift, Saner reminded the Trustees of the highly corrosive atmospheric conditions in the Anderton area and the consequential need for re-painting of the exposed metalwork every third year to counter its effects. Although there is no clear record whether the recommendations were adhered to, it can be assumed that, while Saner remained as the Engineer, they were. In later years, however, painting appears to have been done, at best, once every 4 or 5 years.

During the years leading up to the First World War, the operation and management of the lift were relatively trouble free, although a problem did arise within 5 years or so with respect to the condition of several of the wire lifting ropes on which some of the strands had broken. Investigations revealed that the problem was caused by fatigue failure resulting from the frequent bending and straightening of the ropes as they passed over the pulleys. The longer ropes to the centre of the lift were in poorer condition because they passed over two pulleys, and therefore went through the bending and straightening process twice as often as the shorter ropes. Thereafter, the ropes

In this view, taken circa 1920, both caissons are on the move whilst one of the lift operators looks on from above, near to the control cabin. In 1908, as many as 68 boats a day would pass through the lift with each caisson making around 25 lifts.

The control cabin.

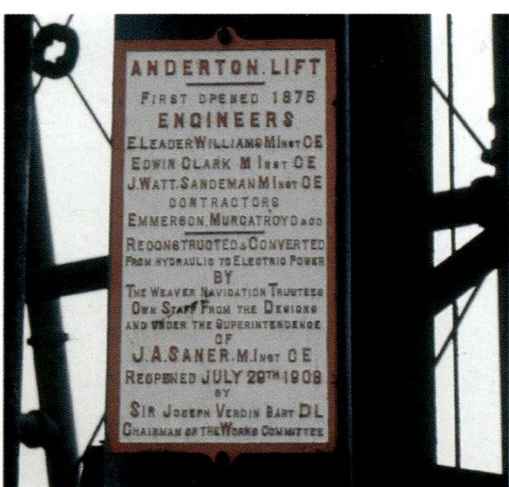

This cast iron plaque on one of the columns records the construction of the hydraulic lift in 1875 and its conversion to electrical operation in 1908.

were inspected on a regular basis with replacement as and when necessary.

The onset of the First World War led to a decline in traffic on the canal system as a whole, which was also reflected in the tonnages being passed through the lift. The canals that, by that time, had been taken over by railway companies were placed under the jurisdiction of the Railway Executive Committee, in order to promote the use of inland waterways in the national war effort. The employees of these canal companies were given protected status and hence excluded from the draft. The other canal companies and private carriers, which presumably included the Weaver Navigation and the Anderton Boat Lift, were not protected in this way and were consequently badly affected, with their employees either enlisting or taking up more lucrative employment in the munitions industry. With an impoverished canal transport system, goods were transferred onto other forms of transport, particularly the railways.

The inter-war period saw business very much as usual for the boat lift, with continued operation and regular maintenance, particularly with respect to the ever-present problem of corrosion. In 1920, the ironwork of the original lift was recorded as being in very good condition but, rather surprisingly, some of the steelwork that was installed in 1908 was found to be corroded and already in need of repair. The following year, the aqueduct and caissons

Some time in the 1930s, a horse-drawn narrowboat leaves the lift into the river basin on its way to collect pottery materials, either from Weston Point or transshipped from a Weaver flat in the river basin at Anderton. The rough state of the boat indicates the hard use it experienced in this trade.

A pre First World War view from outside the control cabin, looking towards the Trent & Mersey Canal, with a narrowboat in the approach aqueduct about to descend. The canal towpath ended at the entrance to the aqueduct and horse boats had thus to be poled across into the caissons.

were inspected and the exposed surfaces were also found to be badly corroded, with the result that extensive repairs were carried out during 1922.

On 10th November 1927, an accident was caused by the lift operator mistakenly applying the safety pawls to an ascending caisson, with the caisson and its contents being brought to an abrupt halt. Fortunately, the damage resulting was not very serious. (The pawls were safety devices that interlocked with the ratchets on the cast iron headgear and were intended for use either when the caissons were being lowered or when static at river level, to avoid the possibility of the motors unintentionally being driven backwards by out-of-balance forces). More serious damage or injury was seemingly avoided by the elasticity of the wire ropes.

New hours of working for the lift were put in place in 1932, which reflected the slowly dwindling volume of traffic using the lift and the canal system as a whole. The new working times were 7 a.m. to 6 p.m. during the months of October, November and March; 8 a.m. to 6 p.m. during December, January and February; and 6 a.m. to 10 p.m. for the months April to September inclusive.

Colonel Saner, who had been the Engineer to the Trust for nearly 50 years, retired in 1934 and was replaced by his assistant C. M. Marsh. The potential implications for the boat lift of the retirement of Saner should not, however, be overlooked. Saner was the designer and constructor of the 1908 electrical lift and would therefore have had a personal interest in ensuring its success. As Engineer to the Trust, Saner was in an influential position to ensure that the ageing structure was given as much attention as it required. It can be argued that, after Saner's retirement, the lift came to be regarded as just another working structure on the Weaver Navigation.

The ensuing years up to the onset of the Second World War saw ongoing repairs and renewals on the lift, frequently to attend to corrosion problems but also including rope replacements and re-painting.

At the start of the war, members of the Local Defence Volunteer Force, (the Home Guard), were detailed to keep the boat lift under observation during night time hours, as it was perceived as a potential target for German attack. The lower grades of staff on the Weaver Navigation were called up for active service and, for the war years at least, the waterway would have been operated with fewer men. The positions held by senior members of staff, including the Lift Attendant, were designated as reserved occupations.

A serious incident took place in 1944 when, for an unidentified reason, a

*Two contrasting photographs of the interior of the control cabin, with 50 years between them. The first view, **top**, was taken in 1931 and shows the Lift Attendant operating the controls for the western caisson. The controls for the eastern caisson are on the left. The second view, **bottom**, taken in the early 1980s, shows the changes in control gear which had taken place over the intervening years. Note these views are looking in opposite directions in the cabin.*

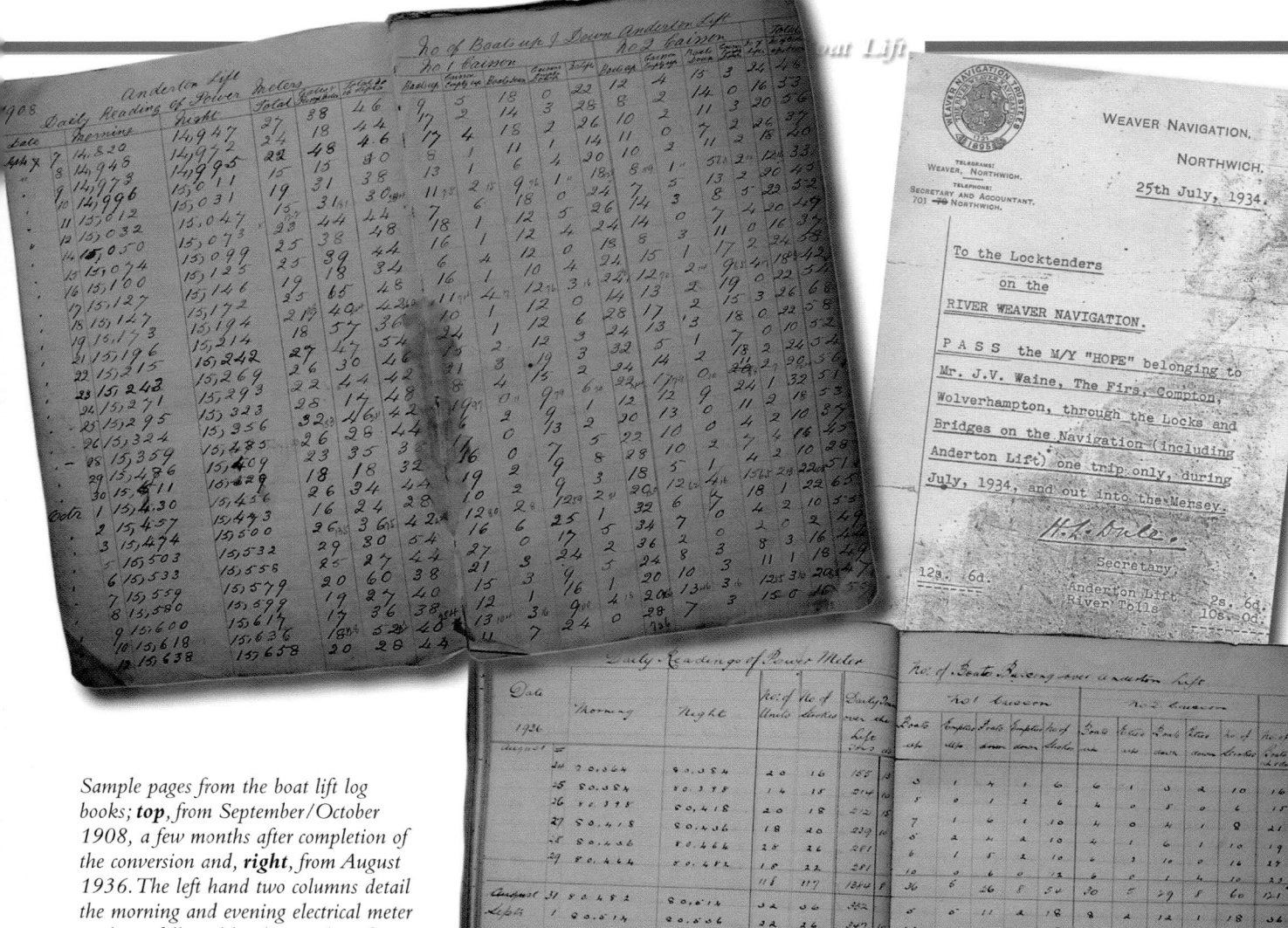

*Sample pages from the boat lift log books; **top**, from September/October 1908, a few months after completion of the conversion and, **right**, from August 1936. The left hand two columns detail the morning and evening electrical meter readings, followed by the number of units used, the daily tonnage, and then the number of boats passed both up and down, loaded and empty, in each caisson. The document, **top right**, is a pass issued in 1934 by the Weaver Navigation Trust, to allow the passage of the motor yacht Hope through the lift and onto the Navigation.*

Left: *Henry Seddon & Sons Limited exported large quantities of salt from their works at Middlewich via the Trent & Mersey Canal and River Weaver. Here one of Seddon's narrowboats is seen transshipping bagged salt into the their steam packet* Weaver Belle *in the basin next to the lift in the early 1950s. Scenes like this could be seen at Anderton until Seddons ceased canal transport in October 1960.*

Below: *A view taken from the bank at the west side of the lift, showing the control cabin and the last remaining salt chute. This was formerly used to transfer the loads of narrowboats from Henry Ingram Thompson's Lion Saltworks at Marston to waiting packets for the trip down river to Runcorn or Liverpool Docks.*

Weaver Belle *departs the Anderton Basin, heading down the River Weaver towards Weston Point.*

A graphic view looking down the inside of the lift in 1969, with a British Waterways maintenance boat descending to river level.

Leaving the westerly caisson onto the aqueduct.

significant amount of water leaked from a caisson whilst it was being lowered; this resulted in the electric motor being driven backwards as the counterweights pulled the caisson back to the top of the lift. The damaged motor was overhauled by British Electrical Repairs Ltd and re-installed six months later. Single caisson working would have been necessary during the intervening period.

In June 1949, as a result of the 1947 Transport Act, the Weaver Navigation Trust was dissolved by the Board of Trade and its functions taken over by the British Transport Commission. Virtually the whole of Britain's transport system, including the roads, railways and inland waterways, were taken into public ownership at the same time. Regrettably, and perhaps not surprisingly, the process of nationalisation did not cure the financial difficulties of the waterways. Whilst various re-organisations of the management structures took place, there was seemingly no new money available which, by that time, was desperately needed to address many years of under-investment. The thirty or so years following nationalisation, leading up to the eventual closure of the boat lift, were to be difficult times for the inland waterways in general, and the Weaver Navigation in particular.

By 1949, the elements of the original hydraulic boat lift that had been retained after conversion to electricity in 1908 were over seventy years old, whilst the remaining elements were generally over forty years old. The passing years and the badly polluted environment at Anderton had both left indelible marks on the boat lift structure. Curiously, the components worst affected by corrosion were those that had been installed in 1908, whilst the older 1875 components had generally fared better. This is largely explained by the state of materials technology at the turn of the century. The principal structural elements in the 1875 lift were the vertical columns and the hydraulic rams beneath the caissons, all of which were fabricated from cast iron, which at that time could be produced to a consistently high quality. Another advantage of cast iron was its high resistance to corrosion. By 1908, however, the construction industry was in the throes of adopting steel, a relatively new material that offered the designer greater freedom of structural form, permitting the use of horizontal beams for large spans where arch construction would previously have had to be adopted. Steel, however, was more vulnerable to corrosion than cast iron.

Another change occurred in 1953, when the inland waterways came under the jurisdiction of the newly formed British Transport Waterways but still in the overall control of the British Transport Commission. By this time, traffic through the lift had dwindled to a handful of commercial boats a day. The 1950s and 60s marked the quietest period in the life of the boat lift, when commercial carrying was coming to an end but the value of the canals for leisure purposes was yet to be realised. As a result, the lift was generally being operated by the Lift Attendant on his own and by the early 1960s it had become normal practice to operate it under continuous single-caisson working.

Yet another re-structuring of the inland waterways took place as a result of the 1962 Transport Act, which led to the abolition of the British Transport Commission on the 1st January 1963 and the creation of the British Waterways Board. The Weaver Navigation, and hence the Anderton Boat Lift, has been under the control of the British Waterways Board, now referred to simply as British Waterways, ever since.

In 1965, after a statutory inspection of the lift, a firm of consulting engineers were commissioned by British Waterways to carry out a detailed structural assessment of the corroded lift structure and aqueduct. They identified many serious defects and made a number of recommendations, including the repair and replacement of badly corroded sections of steelwork and re-painting of the whole structure.

By 1972, the condition of the boat lift was again giving concern and the same firm of consulting engineers were brought in to carry out another detailed assessment of the structure. They reported that the lift was in very poor condition and numerous recommendations were made for urgent repair works. It was suggested that the deterioration had been a gradual process over the seven years since their previous inspection. This was presumably due mainly to the age of the structure but was also perhaps exacerbated by a lack of adequate maintenance and repair. The consultants advised that, unless urgent steps were taken to arrest the corrosion and repair the damaged sections, a major collapse might occur.

Although there is no continuous record of volumes of traffic through the lift after nationalisation, the decline in commercial traffic continued and by the mid 1970s it had all but disappeared. By that time, use of the lift was almost entirely by pleasure craft and boat movements on the waterways had become seasonal in nature. It is probable that the boat lift had been operating at a financial loss since the mid 1960s, with income from tolls being significantly less than the cost of working and maintaining the ageing structure.

In 1976, the Anderton Boat Lift was scheduled as an 'Ancient Monument' by English Heritage under

Empty narrowboats exiting the lift into the Anderton Basin.

By the 1950s, trade had slackened and all bar one of the salt chutes (on the far side of the lift in this view) had been removed. Several flats can be seen in the basin awaiting salt cargoes, whilst the Stanley Arms public house (always known to the boatmen as 'The Tip') is prominent in the background above their masts.

One of the most well known and best remembered images of the boat lift – the cover of the Meccano Magazine of March 1949.

The Anderton Basin from the south bank of the River Weaver circa 1930.

the Town and Country Planning Act. The schedule, rather prosaically, describes the monument in the following way:

'A boat lift connecting the River Weaver to the Trent & Mersey Canal. Built in 1875 as a hydraulic lift, it was converted to electric power during the 20th century. A wrought iron aqueduct carries the canal, which is 50ft above the river, to the two independently operating tanks in which craft are raised and lowered. The structure is still in use and in fair condition.'

An incident, very similar to that in 1944, occurred again in the late 70s, probably in 1978. A caisson was being raised with the end gates leaking badly, possibly due to the poor condition of the metalwork, the rubber seals and lack of maintenance. In the event, the loss of water was sufficient to upset the balanced operation of the caisson, with the consequence that the counterweights took control and accelerated the lift of the caisson to the upper level, causing the electric motor to burn out. Fortunately, apart from the motor, no other damage or injury was incurred.

Perhaps not surprisingly, given the deteriorating condition of the lift structure and the poor financial status of the waterways, other potentially serious incidents occurred around this time. Two resulted in caissons, including boats and passengers, being temporarily stranded part way up the lift. The first, thought to be in 1979, resulted in a narrowboat with two or three crew on board being marooned for a period of around two hours, until fitters from British Waterways' Northwich Repair Yard were able to free one of the safety ropes that had inexplicably become snagged on the structure. In another incident, the lift operator accidentally lowered a gate onto a passing boat; fortunately, there were no injuries and seemingly no significant damage. In yet another incident during the Inland Waterway Association's national rally on August Bank Holiday in 1979, one of the caissons was driven too high causing unspecified structural damage to the lift.

An incident occurred on 14th April 1981, however, which this time had very serious consequences and obvious parallels with the one which had occurred just a few years earlier. The aqueduct end gate of a caisson was not properly closed as the caisson, carrying a narrowboat and passengers, began its descent from the top level. The resulting loss of water from the caisson was such that, after about 6 feet of travel, the counterweights took control and the caisson began moving back up as the lifting ropes lost grip and began slipping through the pulley wheels overhead. At this stage the safety ropes should have fulfilled the purpose for which they had been designed by becoming taut and taking half the counterweights out of the equation, thereby restoring the balanced operation of the caisson. Unfortunately, on becoming loaded, the ends of the safety ropes pulled out of their fixings with the result that the upward movement of the caisson was not checked and it accelerated away until it eventually came to an abrupt halt in collision with the aqueduct end and the overhead machine deck. Major damage was caused to structural members of the lift and the caisson, whilst the passengers in the narrowboat, although shocked, were lucky to escape with only minor injury.

The lift was immediately taken out of service until the cause of the incident had been identified and the extent of damage assessed. In all, the lift was shutdown for seven months, during which time an internal inquiry was undertaken which took statements from various people, including the Lift Attendant, eyewitnesses and specialist investigators.

Sadly, within two years of it being re-opened after the 1981 incident, the final and inevitable decision to close the Anderton Boat Lift altogether was taken, by which time the main structural elements of the boat lift were 73 years old with respect to the 1908 converted lift and 108 years old with respect to the 1875 hydraulic lift. It was therefore not particularly surprising that the ravages of time and the corrosive conditions had taken their toll and the lift declared as structurally unsound. And so in Autumn 1983, after a century of almost continuous operation, the Anderton Boat Lift was finally taken out of service.

A trip boat approaching the lift in the early 1980s. By this date, only the westerly caisson was in use.

Two views of the lift taken not long before its closure in 1983, which also show the approach aqueduct and control cabin in some detail. Note the different colours on the 'A' frames, which would suggest that the structure was in the process of being repainted.

The boat lift and surrounding area in 1989. By this date the lift was out of use and the headgear had been removed – the cast iron wheels can be seen stacked on the river bank alongside it. Winnington Chemical works dominate the river bank opposite, whilst on the right the course of the Trent & Mersey Canal can be followed as it passes the boat lift and heads towards the village of Barnton.

CLOSURE AND RESTORATION

With hindsight, the conversion of the lift to electrical operation in 1908 can only be described as a technical and commercial success. Technically it was a very audacious solution to the ongoing problems of corrosion that were being encountered on the hydraulic lift. Commercially, the income over the 70 years working life of the converted structure, for both the lift and the Weaver Navigation as a whole, must have more than repaid the initial capital expenditure of £25,000.

British Waterways lost little time in addressing the issues, with outside consulting engineers being appointed to investigate alternative schemes for refurbishment. Their brief, initially at least, consisted of the appraisal of four basic options for the lift structure, as follows:

a) Restoration of the lift to its full operational condition with two caissons.
b) Partial restoration of the lift to achieve single-caisson operation.
c) Modification of the lift to modern synchro-lift type of operation with refurbishment of the necessary elements of the lift structure only.
d) Preservation of the lift as a static monument.

The investigations involved structural assessment of the lift structure in its badly corroded condition. The outcome was that several critical elements of the lift, including the 1908 machinery deck support beams and the 'A' frame columns, were identified as being so badly corroded as to give cause for concern with respect to the integrity of the whole lift structure. After detailed assessments, including structural calculations, cost estimates and programming, the consultants recommended the full refurbishment of the structure with strengthening of several of the main machinery deck girders by supplementary steel trusses and the filling of the 'A' frame columns with mass concrete. The estimated cost of this option was £215,000.

Further assessments and investigations followed and, before long, it was revealed that the lift was in even worse condition than originally thought. It was consequently decided to minimise the loading on the weakened 1908 'A' frames by removing the cast iron headgear and electrical equipment from the machinery platform, and lowering the caissons and counterweights to the ground. These works began in November 1987 and took about six weeks to complete. The majority of the items removed from the machinery platform were stockpiled on the ground to the east of the lift, whilst the remainder were taken to the Repair Yard at Northwich for safekeeping.

During 1991 and 1992, British Waterways carried out extensive structural surveys and analyses of the lift structure. One of the objectives was to ascertain how much of the original structure could be retained if the lift was to be

*Two views of the redundant boat lift in 1998 with, **top**, gear wheels stacked on the ground and, **bottom**, the weed filled caissons in the lift chamber.*

This aerial view of the disused lift and the Anderton Basin was taken in 1986 shortly before removal of the headgear. This was taken off so as to lessen the strain on the rest of the structure. A coaster can be seen unloading coal at the Anderton Depot wharf and the Trent & Mersey Canal just appears bottom left.

restored and, consequently, the extent of the replacement works necessary. It was subsequently identified that the likely cost of full restoration of the lift structure had risen to £2.8 million. It should be noted, however, that this estimate related only to the lift structure itself and did not allow for any works that might be needed to the aqueduct and the canal and river basins.

British Waterways formally applied to English Heritage for approval to carry out a full restoration of the electrical lift on 6th July 1994 and consent for the works was duly granted on 3rd October of the same year.

Lewin, Fryer & Partners, based at Hampton in Middlesex, first became involved in the project in November 1994, when they were commissioned by British Waterways to review the feasibility of the proposed works for the full restoration of the electrical lift. The consultants' report concluded that the capital cost of the restoration works would be around £3.5 million, a sum that then included the necessary remedial works to the aqueduct and ancillary structures.

British Waterways' original intention was to restore the boat lift to electrical operation, generally to its condition after conversion to electricity by J. A. Saner in 1908. However, in 1997, British Waterways, in consultation with English Heritage, decided to restore the lift to hydraulic operation, generally as designed by Edwin Clark in 1875, with the 1908 structural elements being retained as a static monument. This decision, however, necessitated

Seen here shortly before restoration commenced, shorn of its headgear and all the ropes and pulleys that went with it, the structure of the 1875 hydraulic lift stands out quite clearly. The supporting 'A' frames, upper deck and control cabin of the 1908 reconstruction straddle the slender ironwork of Edwin Clark's original design.

further investigations and studies in order to identify the conditions of those elements of the hydraulic lift structure that, hitherto, had been neglected, in particular the ram shafts and access tunnels beneath the floor of the lift basin. Consequently, Lewin, Fryer & Partners were commissioned to extend their studies accordingly, with one of the outcomes being that the estimated cost for restoration works rose to £5.5 million.

By March 2000, all the pieces of the jigsaw were finally in place and British Waterways were able to begin the restoration works. For this purpose, temporary project offices were established adjacent to the lift site, from where British Waterways managed and co-ordinated all aspects of the restoration works. The actual design and physical work was generally undertaken by outside consultants and specialist sub-contractors but with British Waterways' Repair Yard at Northwich carrying out some of the more specialised tasks, including the repair and refurbishment of the cast iron headgear of the 1908 electrical lift. The works entailed the dismantling of the 1908 elements of the lift, which were the worst affected by corrosion, and their refurbishment at remote premises; removal of the caissons for extensive refurbishment at the lift site; major modifications to the lift basin to strengthen the foundations for the new hydraulic rams; refurbishment of the remaining elements of the 1875 structure *in situ*, including the cast iron guide columns and the aqueduct; fabrication and installation of modern hydraulic rams and associated equipment; installation of modern control equipment necessary to meet current health and safety standards; and the refurbishment of the canal basin.

The restoration works were successfully carried out over a 2 year period with the lift being officially re-opened on Tuesday 26th March 2002.

Two views of the aqueduct which had become something of a water garden!

ACKNOWLEDGEMENTS

Thanks and credit are due to a number of individuals for providing assistance and illustrations:

Eric Bottomley for the cover painting and for the pencil sketches; Dave Kitching for providing a number of different historic views and the information to go with them; Edward Paget-Tomlinson, Dennis Parkhouse, Tony Hirst and Basil Jeuda for pictures from their collections. Other photographs are of the authors' own taking or from their collections. Thanks also to Marko Nesovic and Harry Carden for the diagrams showing the operating sequence of the 1875 lift, to Ian Pope for the Cheshire waterways map and to Peter Waine for the lift pass.

The following organisations have also been most helpful in providing illustrations:
The Waterways Trust/The Boat Museum Trust; The Salt Museum, Northwich; The Waterways Trust/National Waterways Archive; The Merseyside Maritime Museum; Cheshire Records Office; The Institution of Civil Engineers; The Manchester Ship Canal Company; Jefferson Air Photography.

The cover painting is available as a fine art print, either from the Anderton Exhibition Centre alongside the lift, or direct from the publishers at Unit 144B, Lydney Industrial Estate, Harbour Road, Lydney Gloucestershire GL15 5DD

RESTORATION WORK IN PROGRESS

With the lift initially being almost totally dismantled, much of the refurbishment work was able to be carried out off site, the component parts only being returned once work on them was completed. Everything was then carefully re-assembled and re-erected, with the whole structure being cocooned in a mass of scaffolding, as these assorted views of it show.

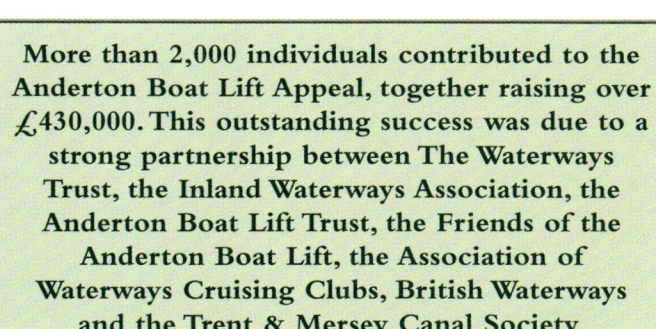

More than 2,000 individuals contributed to the Anderton Boat Lift Appeal, together raising over £430,000. This outstanding success was due to a strong partnership between The Waterways Trust, the Inland Waterways Association, the Anderton Boat Lift Trust, the Friends of the Anderton Boat Lift, the Association of Waterways Cruising Clubs, British Waterways and the Trent & Mersey Canal Society.

OPENING DAY

On 26th March 2002, the special trip boat *Edwin Clark* travelled down river with its 'cargo' of VIPs from British Waterways' depot at Navigation Road, Northwich, to the lift site. It ascended the restored boat lift and the passengers then disembarked at the canal level before the opening ceremony. The lift was formally declared open by Dr David Fletcher, Chief Executive of British Waterways. Also seen on the rostrum are, from left to right; the town crier of Chester, David Mitchell; Roger Hanbury, Chief Executive of the Waterways Trust; Derek Cochrane, North West Regional Director, British Waterways; Martin Bell OBE, former MP for the Tatton Ward and President of the Anderton Boat Lift Appeal; Kate Dixon (hidden), of the Heritage Lottery Fund; and Dr George Greener, Chairman of British Waterways. A cloud of blue and white balloons (British Waterways' colours) were then released, whilst on top of the lift, bright blue windsocks danced a triumphant jig over the proceedings.

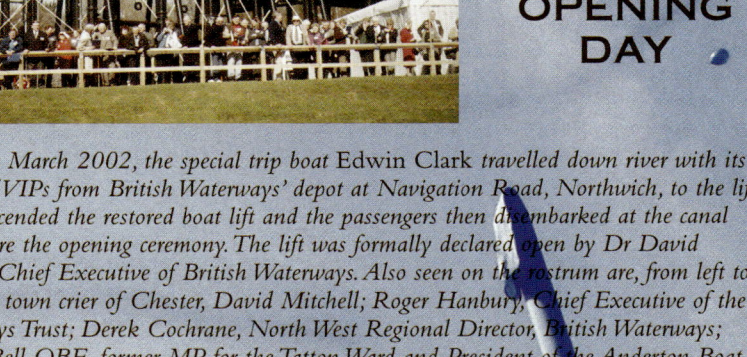

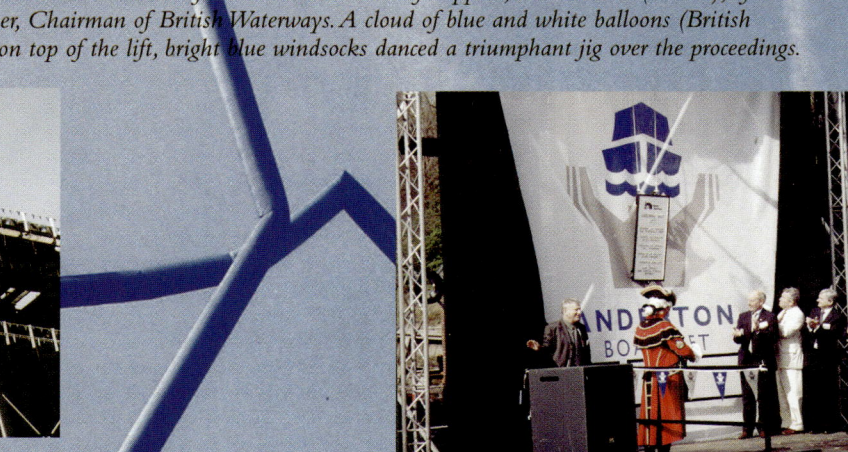

A Guide to the Anderton Boat Lift

1. Approaching the entrance to the lift off the Trent & Mersey Canal.
2. Entering the top basin underneath the footbridge.
3. Top gate open and about to proceed into the caisson.
4. The view from the caisson, looking across the Weaver, with a British Waterways maintenance boat in attendance.
5. Waiting for the bottom gate to open so as to exit the caisson.

Main picture: Floodlit view of the lift just prior to restoration.

RIDING THE BOAT LIFT

45

APPENDIX
TONNAGES CONVEYED THROUGH THE LIFT

The table below gives the tonnages of goods conveyed during the 33 year lifetime of the hydraulic lift, between its opening in July 1875 and its conversion to electrical operation in 1908.

YEAR	TONNAGE	YEAR	TONNAGE	YEAR	TONNAGE
1875	17,028	1886	75,942	1897	169,449
1876	31,294	1887	78,611	1898	186,035
1877	30,886	1888	75,375	1899	186,571
1878	37,363	1889	66,989	1900	181,276
1879	37,874	1890	59,688	1901	177,394
1880	40,097	1891	76,600	1902	177,931
1881	44,847	1892	87,763	1903	191,317
1882	22,066	1893	84,434	1904	191,886
1883	48,339	1894	68,920	1905	191,886
1884	49,722	1895	129,187	1906	192,181
1885	67,783	1896	154,849	1907	166,043

The following points with respect to the recorded annual tonnages are worthy of note:

1875 – The tonnage is for 8 months between July 1875 and March 1876.

1876 – To tempt more traffic through the lift, the Trustees halved the charge on boats using it when the same carrier owned the two boats in one caisson.

1882 – A dramatic downturn in tonnages as a result of a failure on the lift which caused its closure for a period of 6 months or so.

1883 – The annual income to the Weaver Navigation from the lift had risen in 1883 to just under £300. Traffic volumes rapidly recovered from the downturn in the previous years.

1886 – Again, to remain competitive with the canal, the Trustees declared that use of the Anderton Lift was free for those vessels already paying tolls on the River Weaver.

1888 – Another downturn in traffic when salt carriage fell due to Brunner Mond laying brine pipes under the river to their works at Winnington, which faced the lift from the far side of the river.

1895 to **1906** – The volume of goods carried increased erratically during this period reaching a peak of 192,181 tons in 1906.

1875 to **1908** – The total volume of traffic passed through the hydraulic lift in its lifetime was nominally 3.4 million tons, with a yearly average of approximately 103,000 tons.

The annual tonnages of goods conveyed through the lift between 1908, when it was converted to electrical operation, and 1947, when the Weaver Navigation was nationalised, are tabulated opposite.

Year	Tonnage	Year	Tonnage	Year	Tonnage
1908	163,782	1920	90,538	1932	74,165
1909	211,071	1921(Dec)	79,802	1933	69,298
1910	-	1922	97,805	1934	66,622
1911	-	1923	89,756	1935	74,153
1912	-	1924	125,922	1936	72,497
1913		1925	19,962	1937	75,126
1914	213,771	1926	107,134	1938	69,673
1915	200,606	1927	129,960	1939	66,207
1916	166,987	1928	137,316	1940	45,025
1917	133,013	1929	140,042	1941	64,115
1918	105,234	1930	112,596		
1919	72,962	1931	77,785	1947	32,624

The tonnages for the years 1910 to 1913 inclusive are not available but during this period the annual throughput is said to have reached 225,000 tons. Similarly, records are not available for the years 1941 to 1946 but the tonnage carried in 1947 confirms the ongoing decline in the fortunes of the lift. Records of tonnages after 1948 are not available. The following points are of interest:

1908 – The tonnage for 1908 is relatively low as it was affected by the stoppages for the conversion of the lift to electricity and by the period of single caisson working between May and July 1908.

1908 to **1912** – The traffic through the lift continued to grow for several years after its conversion, in spite of competition from the railways.

1914 to **1918** – The First World War led to a decline in traffic on the canal system as a whole, which was reflected in the tonnages being passed through the lift. By the end of the war, traffic passing through the lift had more than halved.

1918 to **1929** – Recovery of traffic on the inland waterways after the First World War was hindered by the Depression and the early stages of development of the road transport system in Britain. Competition from roads continued to grow throughout the next few decades.

1929 to **1947** – A downward trend in traffic volumes was established after 1929, most probably due to the growing dominance of road transport.

1940 to **1945** – During the Second World War, as for the First, there was a decline in traffic on the inland waterways which was reflected in the tonnages passing through the boat lift.

1908 to **1947** – The estimated total tonnage of cargo passing through the converted electrical lift, making reasonable assumptions for the missing data, is nominally 4.4 million tons, with an average annual tonnage of approximately 110,000 tons. In comparison the average annual tonnage passing through the hydraulic lift during 33 years of operation was approximately 103,000 tons.

1949 – At the time of nationalisation, the boat lift was still handling a significant volume of traffic and was, even at that stage, thought to be operating in profit.

A Guide to the Anderton Boat Lift

THE FALKIRK WHEEL

In parallel with the Anderton Boat Lift restoration works, British Waterways embarked on an exciting new project in Scotland to link the Union Canal with the Forth & Clyde Canal at Falkirk by means of a new boat lift, referred to as the Falkirk Wheel. This is the first boat lift to be built in Britain since the Anderton Boat Lift and is a pioneering design consisting of two gondolas, or boat tanks, that counterbalance each other and rotate around a central, horizontal axis. The Falkirk Wheel was formally opened by Queen Elizabeth II on 24th May 2002.